GOSHEN I

MW01600254

Intel from Heaven — Security on Earth

A Prophetic Operations Manual for CEOs, Intercessors, and Kingdom Builders in the Final Hour

Written by Tim Kenner
Founder of Chief Prayer Officer, 3:8 Media Group, and Goshen Intel Group™

"He who dwells in the secret place of the Most High shall abide under the shadow of the Almighty."
— *Psalm 91:1*

In this age of global instability, economic collapse, political deception, and increasing spiritual warfare, the remnant must rise with wisdom from above.

This book is for:

- ⚔️ CEOs under pressure
- 🛡️ Intercessors looking for structure
- 🗺️ Developers moving into new regions
- 🏰 Business leaders seeing strange resistance
- 🗯️ Prophetic warriors called to protect, govern, and build

You're not just called to survive. You're called to **occupy, discern**, and **enforce Heaven's verdicts** in your business, city, and sphere.

Welcome to Goshen Intel Group™ — the prophetic command center for your divine assignment.

Table of Contents

- **B. Daily Declarations for Business Leaders and Intercessors**
- **C. Goshen Region Mapping Template**
- **D. Prophetic Risk Audit Workbook**
- **E. Certification Model for SSO (Spiritual Security Officer)**

Foreword

By Apostle Tim

There are moments in history when Heaven releases not just a message, but a **mandate**.

This book — and the vision behind *Goshen Intel Group™* — is one of those moments.

For years, business leaders, entrepreneurs, and city builders have cried out with questions they couldn't fully articulate:

"Why does it feel like something unseen is sabotaging my company?"
"Why do some regions prosper and others suffer, despite the same market conditions?"
"Why do prayerless agendas seem to thrive — while Kingdom businesses face unrelenting pressure?"

The answer isn't economic.
It's **spiritual.**

We are in a **war over regions, resources, and rulership.**
And most of the Church — and the marketplace — is unequipped to fight.

This is why God raised up the Goshen Intel Group™.

This book isn't just a training manual. It's a **breaker**. A **reformer's tool. A watchman's archive.**
It offers prophetic intelligence, spiritual risk analysis, and tested Heaven-approved protocols for protecting what God has given you — and possessing what's still occupied by darkness.

Like Joseph in Egypt, this blueprint prepares you to discern the season, steward the storehouse, and secure your house from judgment while the world shakes.

Inside these pages, you will learn how to:

- Audit spiritual risks affecting your business, staff, and region
- Intercept demonic activity through prayer technology
- Legally petition Heaven's courtroom to reverse losses and enforce verdicts

- Install a 24/7 prophetic protection protocol over your assignments
- Align your company with the voice of God for supernatural insight and multiplication

Tim Kenner, a prophetic reformer, has walked through the fires of spiritual warfare, region-level intercession, and marketplace transformation. He's not writing theory. He's testifying from trenches most never see. And he is raising up a new breed of prophetic strategist to do what Gideon did — pull down altars and build a **safe place for God's people to prosper**.

If you're reading this, it's not by accident.
This book is a **spiritual activation key**.
It's time to come out of Pharaoh's system — and into Goshen.

Welcome to the frontlines.
Suit up.

– Apostle Tim
(Global Marketplace Voice, Kingdom Builder, Prophetic Strategist)

About the Author

Tim Kenner is a prophetic strategist, spiritual reformer, and founder of *3:8 Media Group*, *Chief Prayer Officer™*, and *Goshen Intel Group™*. His life's mission is to bridge

Heaven and Earth through intercession, revelation, and Kingdom innovation — equipping God's people to build, govern, and protect what Heaven is assigning.

From federal prison to prophetic platforms, Tim's journey is marked by radical deliverance, supernatural encounters, and deep revelation into the unseen war behind world systems. He has authored over 100 books on topics ranging from spiritual warfare and Courts of Heaven protocols to marketplace reform, regional intercession, and end-time prophetic intelligence.

In 2023, God commissioned Tim to become a "spiritual security architect" for businesses, cities, and Kingdom initiatives — launching *Goshen Intel Group*™ as a prophetic intelligence and intercession agency for leaders on the frontlines. He now trains CEOs, intercessors, and apostolic builders to install divine protection, discern spiritual sabotage, and partner with Heaven for legacy-level impact.

Tim lives in Huntington Beach, California, with his family, where he oversees multiple Kingdom ventures, builds altar-to-throne strategies, and fights for regional revival. His heartbeat is to see God's people walk in victory, authority, and unshakable Goshen-level covering — no matter what storm is shaking Egypt.

Introduction

Welcome to Goshen.

Not the place on the map — but the spiritual zone God is building for His people in the midst of global shaking.

In Scripture, Goshen was more than a geographic location. It was a supernatural distinction. While Egypt reeled under plague, pressure, and panic, God's covenant people were untouched. There was light in Goshen when there was darkness everywhere else. There was provision in Goshen while famine spread in the land. There was protection in Goshen while judgment fell all around.

In today's world, we don't just need better strategy — we need better spiritual intelligence. We need divine insight into unseen threats. We need to know what gates are open, what doors must close, and what assignments are active against our lives, families, businesses, and regions.

That's where *Goshen Intel Group™* comes in.

This book isn't just a concept or a collection of ideas — it's a Kingdom operation. It was born from warfare. Built through prophetic revelation. And designed for those who are called to build, lead, and protect something that matters.

If you're a business owner, executive, intercessor, or apostolic leader sensing spiritual resistance — this book is your briefing. If you've ever thought, "Something is off, but I can't put my finger on it," this book is your decoder. If you've longed to build a business, ministry, or movement with Heaven's covering from Day One — this book is your battle plan.

You'll discover:

- How spiritual attacks sabotage companies, contracts, and teams
- What it means to install a spiritual security system over your business
- Why the Courts of Heaven are vital for legal protection and justice
- How to hear prophetic intelligence for your region, industry, or clients
- What it takes to become a **Certified Spiritual Security Officer™** for your company

This isn't about fear. It's about foresight. It's about being proactive in the Spirit, not reactive in the natural. It's about installing a firewall around your destiny — one decree, one petition, one act of obedience at a time.

God is raising up Josephs who don't just interpret dreams — they secure storehouses. Nehemiahs who don't just pray — they build with one hand and war with the other. Apostolic builders who see the blueprint and protect the buildout. You're one of them.

Let's activate Goshen-level protection — and install Heaven's intelligence system in your world.

Welcome to the frontlines.

Chapter 1

The Invisible War in the Marketplace

You're not crazy.

If you've ever felt resistance in your business that made no logical sense...
If key deals fall apart at the last minute...
If sudden confusion, fear, or exhaustion hits your team during crucial breakthroughs...
If things move smoothly for a season — and then chaos erupts out of nowhere...

There's a reason.

It's called **spiritual warfare**, and whether we acknowledge it or not, we are all **in it**.

Most Christian entrepreneurs, CEOs, and business owners have never been taught how to identify spiritual warfare in the workplace — let alone fight it. That's because most of the Church has relegated spiritual warfare to deliverance ministries or Sunday altar calls. Meanwhile, Satan has moved into the **marketplace**, launching full-scale demonic campaigns against businesses, staff, regions, contracts, supply chains, clients, and economies.

The war is already raging.
Most believers are just showing up **unarmed**.

⚔️ The Marketplace Is a Battlefield

The Bible says, "The whole world lies under the sway of the wicked one" (1 John 5:19). This includes **financial systems**, **cities**, **corporations**, and **industries**.

The devil has thrones, gates, and ruling spirits assigned to different mountains of culture. One of his primary targets? **Business and finance.** Why?

Because whoever controls the money controls the movement.
Whoever controls the gates controls the flow.
And whoever controls the economy can manipulate governments, fund wickedness, and enslave generations.

That's why the marketplace is one of the fiercest battlegrounds in the spirit — and most Christians are operating in it with **no intelligence, no covering, and no plan**.

👁 💬 Why You're Experiencing Unseen Attacks

Here are some real symptoms of marketplace-level spiritual warfare:

- **Deals constantly fall apart without explanation**
- **Clients disappear after prophetic moments of advancement**
- **Team members start fighting or quitting in patterns**
- **Sickness, car accidents, or family crises hit key players during breakthroughs**
- **You feel fog, confusion, or heaviness in certain meetings or cities**
- **Money leaks, bank errors, and financial delays become normal**

You may think it's bad luck.
It's not. It's **legal warfare** in the spirit realm.

Every region has gates. Every company has altars — either to God or to something else. And every leader is either operating with Heaven's protection... or Hell's permission.

You're not just facing practical opposition.
You're facing **principalities.**

🧠 Marketplace Warfare Is Strategic — Not Random

In the Bible, Satan didn't just attack churches. He attacked **markets, cities, and commerce**:

- Jezebel used witchcraft to control political and economic systems (2 Kings 9:22)
- Demetrius incited a riot in Ephesus because the gospel disrupted idol-based trade (Acts 19)
- Babylon in Revelation is described as a global trade system fueled by sorcery and blood (Rev. 18)

These are not accidents — they are **blueprints**. And we are living in a time where those blueprints have been digitized, scaled, and enforced through AI, globalism, and regional thrones.

🔐 The Call to Install Goshen-Level Protection

In Exodus, God placed His people in **Goshen**, a protected zone where judgment couldn't touch them. Plagues struck Egypt — but not Goshen. Chaos reigned — but not where God's covenant people dwelled.

Today, God is restoring that **spiritual firewall**.
But it's not automatic.

It must be installed through:

- Prophetic intelligence
- Legal intercession
- Regional discernment
- Courts of Heaven decrees
- Angelic enforcement
- Business repentance and alignment

This is the purpose of *Goshen Intel Group™*: to equip leaders like you to **build protected storehouses**, secure your staff and revenue, discern spiritual risk in real estate and business decisions, and hear Heaven's voice **before the shaking comes**.

🛡 This Is a Wake-Up Call

You're not a CEO by accident.
You're not a builder by mistake.
You've been chosen by God to occupy territory in a time of war.

And He won't let you go into battle without intel.
This chapter is the alarm.
The rest of this book is the briefing.

It's time to see the invisible war — and win it.

Chapter 2

Satan's Strategy Against Business and Cities

The enemy is not chaotic.
He is **calculated**.

While many Christians are casually navigating their business and leadership roles, Satan is working from a centuries-old blueprint: **infiltrate cities, control economies, and corrupt influence at the gates.**

He's not after your products.
He's after your **platform.**
Not just your profit — but your **position.**

🧠 Business Is a Gate

In biblical times, business wasn't done in boardrooms — it happened at the **city gates**. That's where kings, elders, judges, and merchants gathered. To control the gate meant to control what came in and what went out — spiritually, economically, and culturally.

Today's "gates" are places of influence:

- Corporate headquarters
- Tech hubs and media platforms
- Real estate and financial districts
- Political roundtables and investment networks

When Satan targets business, he's targeting **access points** — gates that shape culture, funding, and the flow of values.

If he can control the gate, he can control the **narrative.** If he controls the narrative, he controls the **next generation.**

🕸 The Babylon Blueprint: Corrupt, Enslave, Control

The book of Revelation paints a picture of end-time Babylon — a system of trade, wealth, sorcery, and bloodshed (Revelation 18). This is not just a city — it's a spiritual **network** that touches **commerce, media, politics, and religion.**

This system:

- Corrupts **values** (sorcery = mind control)
- Enslaves **people** (human trafficking, exploitation)
- Controls **wealth** (cursed economies, unjust systems)
- Silences **righteousness** (persecution of truth and prophets)

We see it today in everything from ESG agendas and technocratic surveillance, to woke corporations funding rebellion, to economic models that **reward lawlessness and punish faith.**

This is not random. This is Babylon's **financial warfare.**

🧱 Satan Builds Strongholds with Legal Ground

Satan doesn't work in chaos — he works in **contracts.** He looks for legal ground:

- A bloodline curse that hasn't been broken
- A founder's vow or pact
- Land defiled by sin or idolatry
- A leader who opens the door to fear, greed, or manipulation

Once there's a legal right, the enemy builds a **stronghold** — a structure in the spirit where demons can operate freely.

That's why some companies feel **"cursed"** and no rebranding or reorg can fix it.
The root is **spiritual**, not cosmetic.

Until the **altar is torn down** and the **verdict of Heaven is enforced**, the demonic rights remain.

✉ Why Cities Collapse Without Watchmen

Just like companies, **cities** are spiritually governed.
Every city has gates.
Every gate has watchers.
And every watcher is either on assignment from Heaven
— or from Hell.

When a city lacks prophetic intercession, demonic
policies flourish.
When a region is flooded with sin, bloodshed, or
injustice — demons gain ground.
Without righteous watchmen, businesses inside those
regions become **targets**.

That's why businesses experience waves of:

- Break-ins
- Mental breakdowns
- Drug and homelessness crisis affecting
  customers
- Property value collapse
- Cursed development zones

And yet no one connects it to the **unseen war.**

🛡 Goshen Intel = City-Level Spiritual Defense

This is why *Goshen Intel Group™* was birthed.

We are not just praying for businesses.
We are mapping spiritual risk.
We are filing Court petitions to reverse legal rights.
We are identifying demonic infrastructure — and
dismantling it.

Every prophetic decree.
Every intercessory alert.
Every altar prayer and Watchman Report™
— is designed to restore **righteous dominion** at the
gates.

Because once the city is free,
— the businesses will prosper.
Once the business is cleansed,
— the gate can carry glory again.

This is the devil's strategy.
But God has a **greater one** — and you're part of it.

Chapter 3

Why Prayerless Companies Are Spiritually Unprotected

Let's be blunt:
Prayerless companies are undefended companies.

No matter how sharp the brand...
No matter how excellent the product...
No matter how brilliant the business plan...

If there is **no spiritual defense**, there is **legal exposure in the spirit realm.**

This is not optional.
It is **spiritual law**.

"Unless the Lord watches over the city, the watchmen stand guard in vain."
— *Psalm 127:1*

The same applies to your office building, your supply chain, your revenue streams, and your team.

Without prayer — there is no protection.
Without alignment — there is no authority.

🛑 Why Prayerlessness Invites Demonic Access

Just like an unlocked door invites a thief, a prayerless company gives demons legal grounds to:

- **Interfere with contracts**
- **Destroy internal culture**
- **Attack leadership through temptation or confusion**

- **Create cycles of chaos, theft, and premature failure**

The enemy doesn't need your permission — he needs your **ignorance.**
When there's no watchman in place, Satan assigns one of his own.

This is how witchcraft, confusion, and spiritual sabotage **enter the boardroom.**

Many CEOs don't believe in the supernatural — but demons don't care what you believe.
They care what's **legally permitted.**

🧱 Prayerlessness = Absence of Altar

Every company has an altar — knowingly or unknowingly.

An altar is a **place of exchange:**

- Covenant is made
- Protection is requested
- Agreement is established
- Sacrifice is offered
- Power flows

If a prayer altar to the Lord isn't active in your company, then **other altars** have legal room to operate.

Some examples:

- A founder who once offered a dedication to a false god or spiritualist group
- A team that participates in New Age meditation, astrology, or vision boarding
- A building constructed on defiled land or former occult territory
- A business that profited through exploitation or unjust partnerships

These form **spiritual openings** — and without prayer, no one's watching the gate.

🛡 Prayer Is the First Layer of Spiritual Security

When prayer becomes part of your company culture, you activate:

- **Discernment** to spot spiritual attack before it manifests
- **Covering** over your team, contracts, and physical property
- **Alignment** with Heaven's will for decisions, hiring, finances, and strategy
- **Enforcement** of God's verdicts and angelic assignments

Prayer is not religious.
Prayer is legal.
Prayer is prophetic.
Prayer is **protective intelligence**.

"Surely the Sovereign Lord does nothing without revealing His plan to His servants the prophets."
—*Amos 3:7*

Without prayer, you don't see it coming.
With prayer, you hear **before** the ambush hits.

⚠ Most Businesses Don't Have Intercessors — So Demons Run Unchecked

Let's get real:
Most companies have HR, legal, operations, and marketing...
But they have **no intercessory coverage**, no prophetic counsel, and no spiritual risk awareness.

Meanwhile:

- Witchcraft-practicing CEOs are dedicating their companies to false spirits.
- Global elites are funding movements through demonic covenants.
- Influential brands are releasing curses through advertising and entertainment.

- Occultists are actively astral-projecting into companies to gather information and sow confusion.

And Christians?
They're still debating whether spiritual warfare is "real."

We're behind.
That's why *Goshen Intel Group*™ exists — to **close the gap**.

🔒 Prayer Isn't a Nice Option — It's Your Firewall

You wouldn't leave your bank passwords unprotected.
You wouldn't leave your front door wide open in a bad neighborhood.

So why run your company **without prophetic intelligence and spiritual defense?**

This chapter isn't just a warning — it's a solution.
In later sections, you'll receive:

- Templates to set up prayer altars in your company
- Tools to install spiritual security teams (SSOs)
- Daily declarations and intercession guides for CEOs

- Legal petitions for your business in the Courts of Heaven

You don't need to be a prophet — but you do need to be **covered**.

Because in today's climate, if you're prayerless...
You're already compromised.

Chapter 4

Demonic Gateways: How Altars, Bloodlines, and Agreements Operate Over Regions

Regions are not just **geographic zones** — they are **spiritual battlegrounds**.
Every region has **gateways** — entry points in the spirit realm through which either Heaven or Hell flows.

To understand why some cities thrive in righteousness and peace while others fall into chaos, violence, and collapse, you must first understand this:

Demons need gateways. And gateways require legal access.

Let's expose how those gateways are formed — and how to close them.

△ 1. Altars: The Spiritual Power Stations

An altar is a **spiritual platform of agreement** between the natural and supernatural.

- God's altars release blessing, covenant, and protection.
- Satanic altars release curses, bondage, and bloodshed.

Altars can be built in:

- Families (through generational sin or covenant)
- Land (through bloodshed, idolatry, or dedication)
- Cities (through law, ritual, or structure)
- Corporations (through founding agreements, vows, or idolatry)

Where an altar stands, the **spirit behind it** has legal access.

Example:

- A city with decades of abortion, Freemasonry, or occult festivals will have altars empowering territorial spirits.
- A business headquartered in a defiled region, or dedicated unknowingly to mammon or witchcraft, may carry demonic inheritance until the altar is renounced and dismantled.

"They built high places... and burned their sons and daughters in the fire... which I did not command." – *Jeremiah 7:31*

Altars are **invisible strongholds** unless you have **prophetic eyes**.

🩸 2. Bloodlines: The Inherited Legal Rights

Just like DNA carries traits, bloodlines carry **spiritual inheritances** — both righteous and demonic.

If a person in your business or leadership bloodline:

- Made a vow to a false god (e.g., Freemasonry, Eastern mysticism)
- Shed innocent blood (e.g., abortion, war crimes, human trafficking)
- Practiced witchcraft or sorcery
- Abused spiritual authority or established unjust structures

...then demons can **claim rights** in that family line — and by extension, in that business.

This doesn't just affect one person. It affects:

- Leadership decision-making
- Financial flow

- Succession planning
- Strategic partnerships

Bloodline gates must be closed **legally in the Courts of Heaven**. It is not a matter of willpower — it's a matter of **jurisdiction**.

🤝 3. Agreements: The Contracts That Open the Gate

A demon doesn't need your worship — just your **agreement**.

Spiritual agreements are often made through:

- Words (spoken curses, oaths, or dedications)
- Partnerships (with compromised individuals or networks)
- Rituals (initiation, vision boards, new age meditations)
- Structures (laws, contracts, covenants that go unrepented)

Most businesses don't even realize when they've made these agreements.

Examples:

- Hiring a consultant who operates in witchcraft or New Age
- Partnering with a financier whose wealth is sourced through unrighteousness
- Allowing spiritually compromised individuals to control key leadership roles
- Participating in deceptive branding rooted in occult symbolism

Every agreement is a **yes or no** in the spirit.
Neutrality is not an option.

🏦 Why Regions Carry Spiritual Cycles

This is why some cities and industries get stuck in:

- Cycles of crime and corruption
- Massive fires or natural disasters
- Repeated bankruptcies or collapses
- Inexplicable suicide clusters or addiction epidemics

These are **not coincidences**. They are the result of **unaddressed spiritual gateways.**

Until:

- The altar is torn down
- The bloodline is cleansed

- The agreement is broken
- The verdict is issued in Heaven's Court

...then the demons assigned to that gateway continue to operate freely.

🛡 Goshen Intel Assignment: Find and Close the Gates

One of the core assignments of *Goshen Intel Group*™ is to:

- **Identify demonic gateways over companies and regions**
- **Disrupt the enemy's legal access**
- **Seal the gates with righteous intercession, decrees, and verdicts**

That's why we train business leaders in:

- How to spiritually map their region
- How to conduct risk audits and altar investigations
- How to close bloodline gates and break unrighteous covenants
- How to protect their land, team, and contracts from spiritual invasion

Because **where altars fall, angels rise.**
And where Jesus is enthroned, no devil can rule.

Chapter 5

Spiritual Espionage: When Witchcraft Enters the Boardroom

Most people think of corporate espionage in terms of stolen files or insider leaks.
But there's a **deeper espionage at work** — one that's harder to detect and far more dangerous.

It's **spiritual espionage**.
And it's happening in **boardrooms, Zoom calls, contracts, and strategic partnerships**.

Behind the scenes of billion-dollar companies and startup incubators, there are:

- **Witches and warlocks posing as consultants**
- **New Age energy workers hired for "culture elevation"**
- **Executives practicing manifestation, astrology, and psychic insight**
- **Occult altars operating beneath the surface of HR programs and DEI initiatives**

This isn't superstition.
It's **the enemy's stealth warfare strategy** — and the church has barely noticed.

🕵️ Witchcraft in the Workplace: What It Looks Like

Witchcraft in business isn't just people casting spells. It often looks like:

- Vision boards rooted in universalism and "law of attraction"
- Meditation rooms promoting Kundalini or chakra alignment
- Executive coaches using pendulums, spirit guides, or Tarot
- DEI trainings that invoke ancestral worship or spiritual rituals
- Business books that teach how to "channel energy" for success

What's the problem?
Every counterfeit spirit brings an invitation.

You may think you're hiring a strategist — but you just gave legal access to a sorcerer.

You may think you're upgrading your culture — but you're actually **building an altar to demons**.

💼 Demonic Assignments Through People

Spiritual espionage often comes **through a person sent on assignment**:

- A new employee who is friendly, competent — and fully initiated into witchcraft
- A consultant with elite credentials and a secret tie to a Masonic lodge
- A marketing director who incorporates sigils or occult numerology into brand materials
- An investor who gained wealth through trafficking, rituals, or Babylonian systems

These people aren't always conscious infiltrators. But the **spirits operating through them** are.

And once they enter your company:

- The altar of the Lord is challenged
- The anointing lifts
- Confusion increases
- Hidden sabotage begins

It can manifest as:

- Leadership division
- Random health issues
- Employee mental breakdowns
- Sudden financial losses
- Prophetic silence or dullness

And it's not random — it's **spiritual warfare from the inside.**

✳️ The Jezebel Protocol: Witchcraft + Control + Seduction

In Revelation 2, Jesus rebukes the church for **tolerating Jezebel**, a spirit that:

- Calls herself a prophet
- Teaches and seduces
- Leads people into spiritual compromise
- Operates through control, manipulation, and deception

This is the **spiritual blueprint** for how witchcraft operates in organizations.

Symptoms of a Jezebel infiltration:

- A strong, charismatic personality begins dominating leadership

- True prophets and discerning people feel spiritually "foggy" or sick
- Control becomes more valued than character
- Truth is sacrificed for appeasement
- Division replaces unity, and fear replaces faith

If you sense this, you're likely already in **a spiritual war for your company's soul**.

✍ How to Expose and Expel Spiritual Espionage

Here's what the Goshen Intel model teaches clients:

1. **Conduct a Spiritual Risk Audit**
   a. Use our templates to assess contracts, people, land history, and influence channels.
   b. Ask: Who's influencing leadership decisions? What do they believe?
2. **Check for Hidden Altars and Agreements**
   a. Were any founders involved in Freemasonry, witchcraft, or cult activity?
   b. Has the company engaged in public ritual (e.g., blood ceremonies, ancestral dedications)?
3. **Test the Spiritual Atmosphere**
   a. Is prayer easy or hard?

    b. Is worship resisted or received?

    c. Do discerning believers feel peace or pressure?

4. **Deploy Prophetic Intelligence**

    a. Ask the Lord for insight: Who or what is the open door?

    b. Bring in a tested prophetic team if necessary.

5. **Dismantle, Remove, Cleanse**

    a. Fire those on assignment, break ungodly agreements, cleanse the space physically and spiritually.

    b. Replace the defiled altar with **a prayer altar dedicated to Jesus.**

🚨 Spiritual Blindness Is Not an Excuse

You may not have known.

But the enemy has no sympathy for ignorance.

What you **don't know** will be **used against you.**

That's why *Goshen Intel Group™* exists:

To **see what you can't see,**

To **close what you didn't open,**

And to **cover what you're called to build.**

Because in this hour, only companies led by spiritual intelligence — **and governed by righteousness** — will survive the shaking.

Chapter 6

Goshen in Egypt — God's Original Security Protocol

When God wanted to protect His covenant people in the midst of a collapsing world system, He didn't build a bunker.
He gave them **a territory**.
A place within a hostile nation that would become a **supernatural zone of protection, provision, and peace**.

That place was **Goshen**.

"Only in the land of Goshen, where the children of Israel were, there was no hail."
— *Exodus 9:26*

In the greatest economic collapse and judgment in Egyptian history, Goshen became:

- A **spiritual firewall** against plagues
- A **prophetic container** for covenant legacy

- A **geographic intercession zone** that marked the people of God
- A **prototype of Heaven's insurance policy** for the righteous

And now — in these last days — God is **reinstalling the Goshen blueprint.**

Not just for families and churches,
But for **businesses, regions, and entire nations.**

🛡 Goshen Was a Supernatural Exemption Zone

While Egypt collapsed under judgment:

- Israel thrived in Goshen
- Livestock survived
- Light remained
- Children were safe
- Not a single house fell to death or destruction

This wasn't because of better economics.
It was because of **better alignment.**

Goshen wasn't just a location — it was a decision.
A covenantal obedience to stay under God's jurisdiction while judgment fell elsewhere.

♀ Goshen in the Modern Marketplace

What does Goshen look like now?

It looks like:

- A business led by prayer and prophetic insight
- A company that refuses to bow to Babylon's systems
- A team that walks in repentance, intercession, and spiritual integrity
- A CEO who welcomes the Holy Spirit into board meetings, hiring decisions, and contracts
- A real estate development covered by altars of righteousness

It's not about retreat — it's about **rulership in alignment with Heaven.**

Wherever there's Goshen, there is:

- **Preserved wealth**
- **Protected families**
- **Prophetic visibility**
- **Divine justice**
- **Strategic exemption from regional curses**

🌍 Goshen Is Reemerging Through Kingdom Business

As economic collapse, demonic agendas, and global manipulation increase, **God is raising up Goshen companies** — businesses that:

- Hear from Heaven
- War in the Spirit
- Operate in righteousness
- Build altars of purity, not profit-idolatry
- Serve as beacons of Kingdom culture in the economic battlefield

He is **releasing new blueprints** to CEOs, founders, investors, and intercessors.

The enemy is launching counterfeit cities of AI surveillance and Luciferian economics — but the Lord is establishing **prophetic zones of justice, wealth, and holy fire.**

🔐 Goshen Is Not Automatic — It Must Be Installed

You don't stumble into Goshen.

You must:

- **Discern the call**
- **Sanctify the space**
- **Cleanse the atmosphere**
- **Install intercession protocols**
- **Break demonic altars tied to past owners, partnerships, or covenants**
- **Establish legal jurisdiction in the Courts of Heaven**

That's what this book is giving you — a **map to install Goshen** over your business.

Because the shaking is not coming — it's here.
And companies who are aligned with Babylon will fall.
But Goshen businesses will stand — **and thrive.**

🚨 God's Question: Are You Willing to Build Goshen?

Goshen isn't glamorous.
It doesn't always look like Wall Street success or Silicon Valley hype.

But Goshen is:

- Sustainable
- Protected
- Prophetic

- Spiritually firewalled
- Overflowing with divine strategy and provision

If you're reading this, you're not called to build just another brand.
You're called to build **a safe zone for Heaven on earth.**

A modern Goshen.
For your family.
For your staff.
For your city.

Let's build it.

Chapter 7

Prophetic Intel 101: How to Hear from Heaven for Cities and Companies

In war, intel is everything.
And in spiritual war, the most dangerous leader is not the one without power —
It's the one **without sight.**

"Where there is no prophetic vision, the people cast off restraint."
— *Proverbs 29:18*

In this hour, business leaders don't just need better data.
They need **prophetic intelligence** — Heaven's perspective on earthly situations.

It's not optional.
It's the **difference between Goshen and Egypt**, breakthrough and bondage, preservation and collapse.

♟ What Is Prophetic Intel?

Prophetic intelligence is **real-time revelation from God** that:

- Reveals hidden motives, threats, and opportunities
- Exposes demonic traps before they manifest
- Provides strategy, warning, and wisdom
- Aligns decisions with divine timing
- Builds a firewall against unseen spiritual agendas

This isn't fortune-telling or flaky "good vibes."
This is **the strategic edge of the Kingdom of God.**

🧠 Why CEOs Must Become Prophetic

In the Old Testament, kings surrounded themselves with prophets.
Not to feel spiritual — but to **survive and win**.

David had Gad.
Hezekiah had Isaiah.
Jehoshaphat listened to Micaiah over 400 false prophets — and it saved a nation.

Today, CEOs are more likely to surround themselves with analysts, AI, and consultants.

But where are the prophets?

A prophetless boardroom is a boardroom at risk.

If you don't have prophetic insight over your business, city, or region —
You are building blind.

⚒️ Five Ways God Releases Prophetic Intel

Here's how Heaven often downloads strategic insight:

1. **Dreams**
   a. Night visions are often warnings, blueprints, or confirmations.

      b. Keep a dream journal and invite interpretation.

2. **Impressions / Knowing**

      a. Sudden clarity, urgency, or resistance can be the Spirit's direction.

      b. Trust the holy "check" — not every open door is from God.

3. **Scripture Revelation**

      a. God will illuminate verses in perfect alignment with your business decisions.

      b. The Word is the ultimate filter for any prophetic word.

4. **Prophetic Voices**

      a. God sends tested, accurate prophets with messages for businesses and regions.

      b. We vet them. You should too.

5. **Prayer and Fasting Downloads**

      a. Extended prayer often reveals hidden warfare, regional assignments, and divine timing.

      b. Fasting clears the static of carnal voices.

🔍 How to Use Prophetic Intel in Business

A Goshen CEO uses prophetic intel to:

- **Decide where to expand — and where to retreat**
- **Break ungodly partnerships before they poison the culture**
- **See spiritual warfare coming before it hits the bottom line**
- **Navigate volatile markets without panic**
- **Prepare teams with divine assignments, not just job descriptions**

It also means:

- Don't launch a campaign if God hasn't confirmed it.
- Don't hire someone just because their resume is strong — discern their spirit.
- Don't sign contracts without a Courts of Heaven review.
- Don't buy land until you've mapped the region spiritually.

👂 Training Your Ear to Hear

You are not just a CEO — you are a **prophetic gatekeeper**.

To hear from Heaven:

- **Spend daily time with the Lord**, not just reviewing KPIs.
- **Consecrate your business** as a place of His presence.
- **Repent for past reliance on the world's system.**
- **Ask God to speak — then wait.**

If you train your ear, you will become **unstoppable in the Spirit.**

Because prophetic leaders aren't just reacting.
They're **preempting, positioning, and prevailing.**

🔐 Heaven Is Not Silent — You're Being Recruited

God is not withholding insight.
He's looking for someone willing to act on it.

Prophetic intelligence isn't reserved for pastors and prophets.
It's for **every Kingdom leader called to take ground.**

So what will you build with the intel He gives?

The question isn't "Can you hear from God?"
The real question is — **will you obey when you do?**

Chapter 8

Courts of Heaven Protocols for Business, Staff, and Contracts

Your business is not just a brand — it's a legal entity in the spirit realm.

And in times of spiritual warfare, **courtrooms are more powerful than battlefields**.

Many business leaders are praying from the battlefield when they should be **petitioning from the courtroom**.

"For the Lord is our Judge, the Lord is our Lawgiver, the Lord is our King; He will save us."
— *Isaiah 33:22*

The Courts of Heaven are not a metaphor — they are a **divine legal system** where justice is rendered, accusations are overturned, and verdicts are enforced.

If you don't understand how to operate in the Courts, **you'll keep getting attacked with no recourse**.

⚖️ Why the Devil Attacks Through Legal Claims

The enemy is a legalist.

He uses:

- **Unrepented sin**
- **Illicit contracts**
- **Broken covenants**
- **Bloodline curses**
- **Unrighteous partnerships**

...as **legal grounds** to accuse, afflict, and sabotage.

You might fire a toxic employee, cancel a contract, or shut down a project — but if the **spiritual legality** isn't addressed, the enemy still has access.

This is why deliverance sometimes doesn't last.
It's why business breakthroughs get delayed.
Because **the accusation in the courtroom was never silenced.**

📃 The Role of the Courts of Heaven in Business

The Courts are where:

- **Accusations are brought by the enemy (Revelation 12:10)**
- **Jesus acts as our Advocate and Mediator (1 John 2:1)**
- **The Father renders judgment based on covenant alignment**
- **Angels are dispatched to enforce verdicts (Psalm 103:20)**

If your business has experienced:

- Constant financial loss
- Cycles of confusion and conflict
- Partnerships that turn demonic
- Lawsuits with no natural explanation
- Sudden employee moral failure
- Mysterious opposition on specific land or buildings

Then you may need to **present a case in the Courts of Heaven.**

📋 How to File a Courtroom Petition for Your Business

Step 1: Ask the Holy Spirit for Discovery

- "Lord, what legal access does the enemy have?"

- Listen for names, dates, contracts, or sins.

Step 2: Renounce and Repent

- Identify specific sin or unjust agreement.
- Repent on behalf of yourself, team, or bloodline.
- Break word curses, idolatry, or soul ties involved.

Step 3: Present the Case

- Appeal to the blood of Jesus.
- Submit evidence of repentance and alignment.
- Request judgment against demonic assignments, covenants, or curses.

Step 4: Receive the Verdict

- Ask for a righteous ruling from the Judge.
- Ask for angelic enforcement.
- Seal the case with thanksgiving and worship.

Step 5: Enforce on Earth

- Declare the verdict aloud.
- Remove physical objects or partnerships tied to the claim.
- Install prayer covering or anoint physical locations.

📝 Real-Life Applications

Here are some scenarios where this works powerfully:

1. Toxic Contracts

A media company signed with a high-level production firm that seemed like a blessing — until everything unraveled. Turns out the firm had spiritual roots in Freemasonry. The CEO revoked the contract, repented in court, and instantly felt peace return.

2. Land That Fights You

A developer bought property for expansion. Everything failed — permits, employees, unexpected legal threats. In the Courts, it was revealed the land was once a site of abortion rituals. A petition was filed, the blood was renounced, and the atmosphere shifted within 48 hours.

3. Employee Oppression

A prayer-led staff member was under constant attack. In court, it was revealed she had unhealed wounds and a soul tie with a past employer who operated in witchcraft. The tie was severed, and clarity came.

◎ Don't Just Pray — Legislate

You are not just a business owner.
You are a **legal representative of the Kingdom of Heaven** in the marketplace.

Stop begging God to intervene.

Start appearing before Him as Judge.
Present your case.
Overturn the enemy's claims.
Secure righteous verdicts.

The Courts of Heaven aren't for the "deep prophets."
They're for the CEOs, founders, and investors who realize:

This war is legal — and so is your victory.

Chapter 9

Spiritual Risk Audits: Discerning Legal Rights, Hidden Altars, and Demonic Cycles

You wouldn't buy a building without an inspection.
So why run a business without a **spiritual audit**?

Too many leaders invest in legal teams, cybersecurity, and accounting firms—
but ignore **spiritual vulnerabilities** that are the real cause of breakdown, delay, and disaster.

This chapter equips you to **see the unseen liabilities** in your company, staff, land, and contracts—so you can shut the doors to darkness **before** the next crisis.

"Lest Satan should take advantage of us; for we are not ignorant of his devices."
— *2 Corinthians 2:11*

📊 What Is a Spiritual Risk Audit?

A Spiritual Risk Audit is a systematic scan of your business to identify:

- **Open doors** (sin, agreement, unrepented access points)
- **Legal rights of demonic entities**
- **Generational or bloodline curses affecting land or people**
- **Occult influence through prior ownership, events, or covenants**
- **Patterns of spiritual attack (cycles, dates, employee turnover, financial hits)**

It's like a due diligence report—
but in the Courts of Heaven and by the Spirit of God.

🧠 Why Every Kingdom Business Needs One

You might have:

- A pure heart
- A great vision
- A strong strategy

But if the **enemy has legal rights**, you'll hit walls you can't explain.

Examples:

- You open a new branch in a city—and revenue collapses.
- A new hire brings moral confusion into your culture.
- Investors are interested—until the final call.
- Contracts mysteriously dissolve at the finish line.
- The same issue arises at the same time every year.

That's not just bad business.
That's a **demonic cycle** attached to a spiritual claim.

📑 How to Conduct a Spiritual Risk Audit

Use this process quarterly, or whenever facing major business decisions.

1. Pray for Discovery

- "Holy Spirit, reveal any hidden altars, covenants, or legal claims the enemy is using."
- Wait for impressions, names, locations, time frames.

2. Investigate Past Events and Land History

- Was this office space formerly used for occult, abortion, Freemasonry, or false religion?
- Were there past bankruptcies, lawsuits, or betrayals on this land?
- Who previously owned or founded the company?

3. Assess Spiritual Patterns

- When did attacks start?
- Is there a cycle (same time each year or quarter)?
- Are employees experiencing shared affliction (sickness, confusion, fear)?

4. Audit Team and Contracts

- Who has unhealed trauma, open sin, or ties to spiritual darkness?
- Are there contracts, vendors, or partnerships with unclean agendas?
- Is there Jezebel or Leviathan activity operating through communication breakdown, pride, or manipulation?

5. Check for Idolatry or Disobedience

- Have you made business decisions without consulting the Lord?
- Is any area of the business being elevated above obedience?
- Are you tolerating something God told you to remove?

♀ Common Hidden Risks

Risk Category	Symptoms
Bloodline Curses	Chronic financial instability, repeated employee betrayal
Unrepented Sin	Confusion, fog, blocked creativity
Defiled Land	Unexpected legal issues, health problems
Occult Influence	Nightmares, strange presence, tech malfunctions
Unequally Yoked Partners	Division, stagnation, moral decay

✳ What to Do with What You Find

Repent, Renounce, Replace:

1. **Repent** on behalf of yourself or others tied to the business.
2. **Renounce** the legal right — break the contract, curse, or altar.
3. **Replace** it with Kingdom decrees, communion, oil, and worship.

You may need to:

- **Anoint your office and land.**
- **Fire a spiritually compromised employee.**
- **Destroy cursed objects or documents.**
- **Go to the Courts of Heaven and demand judgment against demonic assignments.**

🔐 Don't Just Diagnose — Deliver

A spiritual risk audit is not just about identifying problems.
It's about **closing every door the enemy is using to harass, hinder, or delay.**

You are not just a CEO.
You are a spiritual gatekeeper.

And gatekeepers don't allow access to the wrong kingdom.

Chapter 10

Deploying Angels, Dismantling Darkness, and Enforcing Verdicts

You've discerned the risk.
You've exposed the legal rights.
You've repented, renounced, and revoked.
Now it's time to **enforce the verdict** and deploy Heaven's army.

"Are they not all ministering spirits sent forth to minister for those who will inherit salvation?"
— *Hebrews 1:14*

Many leaders stop at revelation.
Few go on to **activation** — and that's where battles are won.

🕊 What Happens After a Verdict Is Rendered?

When you win a case in the Courts of Heaven:

- **The enemy is stripped of legal rights.**

- **A verdict is released from the Righteous Judge.**
- **Angels are assigned to enforce it.**

But Heaven's verdict must be **enforced on Earth** — by your voice, your authority, and your obedience.

⚔ Step 1: Deploy the Angels Assigned to Your Case

You don't worship angels. You don't command them outside God's will.
But you can **agree with the courtroom verdict**, speak it aloud, and release angelic enforcement.

Example Activation:

"By the authority of Jesus Christ, I release the angels assigned to enforce this verdict.
I command every demonic structure, resistance, or retaliation to be dismantled.
Angels of the Most High, execute your assignment now over this company, over this land, and over this region."

Faith-filled words are a divine dispatch.

🧱 Step 2: Dismantle Demonic Structures in the Spirit

Once verdicts are rendered, the enemy often tries to **delay or resist** enforcement.

That's when you go to war — not in panic, but in **precision**.

Use declarations like:

"Every structure of Jezebel, Leviathan, Python, or Mammon influencing this company — I command you to collapse.
I break the agreement, dismantle the altar, and revoke all demonic assignments.
Let fire from Heaven consume every counterfeit throne.
Let angels destroy and scatter every unholy alliance."

Back it with **worship, communion, and prophetic acts** (e.g., anointing oil, tearing up contracts, renaming places, etc.).

📜 Step 3: Reinforce with Decrees and Altars

Once a structure falls, it must be **replaced with God's government**.

- **Establish a prayer altar** in your company.

- **Take communion regularly over the business.**
- **Write and speak decrees daily.**

Decree examples:

"This company is a Goshen Zone — protected, anointed, and governed by Heaven."
"Every contract, staff member, and dollar is aligned with righteousness and Kingdom purpose."
"We do business under the blessing of Abraham, not the curse of Babylon."
"No witchcraft, retaliation, sabotage, or accusation can stand. The blood speaks louder."

🔁 Step 4: Check for Retaliation — and Shut It Down

Sometimes, darkness strikes back.
You may feel:

- Sudden heaviness or confusion
- Relationship strain or slander
- Dreams of war, snakes, seduction, or fear
- Physical fatigue or chaos in your schedule

Don't be surprised. Be prepared.

Declare immediately:

"I break all backlash and retaliation. I bind every monitoring spirit, lying spirit, and marine spirit.
I declare full covering over my family, team, and territory — by the blood of Jesus."

If needed, go back into the Court and **petition for a gag order, restraining order, and full financial restitution**.

▓ Final Thought: You're Not Just Free — You're Commissioned

Dismantling darkness isn't just about staying safe.
It's about **reclaiming ground** — and **occupying it** until He comes.

You are not just surviving demonic attack —
You are now a **territorial enforcer of God's government.**

Speak like it.
Pray like it.
Build like it.

And let every demon, altar, and unclean structure know:
A Goshen CEO is in the land.

Chapter 11

The Watchman's Report™: Mapping Regional Warfare and Blessing

"I have set watchmen on your walls, O Jerusalem; they shall never hold their peace day or night."
— *Isaiah 62:6*

You don't just need insight for your company.
You need it for your **region.**

Because sometimes, your battles aren't about your business.
They're about the land it sits on.

Cities have strongholds. Regions have rulers. Territories have thrones.
And if you don't know the climate you're building in, you're flying blind.

That's why we developed **The Watchman's Report™** —
A tool to equip business leaders, developers, and intercessors to **see what Heaven sees** about the regions they're assigned to.

✸ Why Regions Matter in Business Warfare

Every territory carries:

- **Spiritual altars** (past agreements or bloodshed)
- **Demonic strongholds** (powers ruling through culture or history)
- **Prophetic promises** (Heaven's assignment over the land)
- **Blessings and judgments** (depending on what's been sown or tolerated)

When you enter a city, you're not just entering a **market**.
You're entering a **spiritual jurisdiction**.

Knowing the **climate** allows you to pray strategically, hire wisely, build prophetically, and **occupy without delay**.

🔍 What's Inside a Watchman's Report™

Each Watchman's Report includes:

- **Spiritual Climate Assessment**
  - Is the region under blessing or judgment?
  - Is there witchcraft, idolatry, freemasonry, bloodshed, or religious manipulation?

- **Demonic Gateways**
  - Identifies highways, institutions, and industries influenced by darkness
  - Exposes hidden thrones (e.g. Jezebel in media, Mammon in finance, Leviathan in government)
- **Historical Curses or Covenants**
  - Uncover where the enemy was invited (abortions, slavery, massacres, cults)
- **Active Angelic Assignments**
  - What has Heaven dispatched?
  - Where are the open portals for revival and favor?
- **Regional Warfare Intelligence**
  - Recent riots, false flags, economic shifts, strange weather, and prophetic patterns
- **Prayer Assignments**
  - Tactical decrees, communion instructions, and angelic activation blueprints

🧠 Sample Application: Los Angeles, California

Let's say your business is headquartered in L.A. You should know:

- **Stronghold**: Jezebel and Mammon (entertainment + wealth without worship)
- **Demonic Gateways**: Hollywood, Santa Monica, specific "sacred geometry" gridlines
- **Historical Curses**: Occult foundations, sacrifices during film booms, LGBTQ altars
- **Blessings**: End-time evangelism hub, Azusa Street residue, Kingdom creatives
- **Assignments**: Raise up Goshen business sanctuaries to oppose Baal systems

So you wouldn't just hire based on résumé.
You'd **discern spiritual loyalty, contracts, and intercession needs**.

🗺️ Building Your Own Watchman's Report

Here's how to do it for any city:

1. Pray for Revelation

- "Holy Spirit, show me the spiritual history and atmosphere over this land."

2. Research Natural and Spiritual History

- Local history, founding fathers, major events, old maps, and indigenous roots

- Study revivals and disasters — both mark spiritual territory

3. Discern Demonic Rulers

- Use dream patterns, discernment, and prophetic voices
- Look for signs of Jezebel (control, seduction), Leviathan (confusion, division), Mammon (greed, idolatry), Python (witchcraft, restriction)

4. Mark the Map

- Identify key altars (abortion clinics, temples, masonic lodges, towers)
- Identify redemptive gates (revival sites, Kingdom businesses, pure churches)

5. Create Prayer Assignments

- Issue decrees to close gates, destroy thrones, and claim inheritance
- Activate your staff, clients, or intercessors with prophetic tasks

◗ Use the Report to Secure Your Business

Once you know the regional climate:

- **Choose locations with angelic movement, not just cheap rent**
- **Set up altars of worship where thrones of Baal used to sit**
- **Pray over city councils, regional events, and infrastructure**
- **Use the map in intercession to claim and cleanse zones**

You're not just making money.
You're **governing gates.**

You're not just building a brand.
You're **installing a fortress of Heaven** in contested territory.

Final Word

The Watchman's Report isn't just prophetic homework.
It's a **spiritual radar system** for your assignment on Earth.

Let the intercessors map.
Let the prophets see.
Let the CEOs **occupy the gates**.

The Kingdom is not coming later.
It's being enforced now.

Chapter 12

The Warfare Vault™: Tools, Templates, and Tactical Decrees for Real-Time Warfare

"For the weapons of our warfare are not carnal, but mighty through God to the pulling down of strongholds."
— *2 Corinthians 10:4*

There is a vault in Heaven.
And inside it are **battle-tested blueprints**, prophetic weapons, and legal decrees that Heaven is ready to release — to businesses, leaders, and intercessors who will **pray strategically, not randomly.**

The **Warfare Vault™** exists to provide those weapons.
No more guessing. No more scrambling in the dark.
This is **real-time Kingdom intelligence and tactical precision.**

⚔ Why You Need a Warfare Vault

Most business owners aren't losing money because of bad marketing.
They're losing because of **unseen interference.**

Here's what the Warfare Vault™ is designed to counter:

- **Staff sabotage and betrayal**
- **Sudden loss of momentum**
- **Demonic interference in key contracts**
- **Generational curses affecting leadership**
- **Witchcraft launched through competitors or former partners**
- **Accusations, lawsuits, or slander from hell's courtroom**

When these hit, you need **spiritual weapons on command.**

Not just prayer — **precision decrees, verdicts, and protocols.**

🧩 What's Inside the Warfare Vault™

Each Warfare Vault™ drop includes assets like:

📒 Courts of Heaven Petitions for Business Scenarios

- Loss of income or clients
- Backstabbing or disloyalty
- Lawsuits or government interference
- Cursed properties or partnerships
- False accusations or reputation sabotage

📅 Daily Warfare Calendars

- PDF and audio-based declarations for each day
- Categories: finances, contracts, staff, protection, restoration
- Bonus: Communion instructions for breakthrough

🗣 Prophetic Altar Prayers

- Prayers to build or restore altars in your business
- Includes repentance, cleansing, dedication, and covering steps

🛡 Angelic Deployment Protocols

- Scripture-based strategies to release angels for protection, escort, justice, and exposure
- Verbal activation prayers with timing instructions (e.g. dawn, midnight watch)

📖 Regional Clean-Up Warfare Templates

- Identify, cleanse, and redeem business properties or project sites
- Includes altar history worksheet, spiritual mapping guide, and land dedication prayers

🔓 Sample Scenario: Business Under Attack

Symptom: Multiple clients cancel without explanation.
Diagnosis: Check for slander, witchcraft, or unrepented altars in the land or leadership.
Solution:

- File a **Court of Heaven Petition for Sabotage and False Accusation**
- Pray the **"Angel of Exposure" deployment decree**
- Conduct a **Repentance + Renunciation altar prayer** as a leadership team
- Use the **"Restore the Client Flow" prophetic declaration set** for 7 days
- If needed, activate **The Midnight Strike**: a prophetic act of warfare prayer between 12–3 AM

The Warfare Vault gives you **battle plans, not just pep talks**.

🔓 What Makes It Effective?

1. **It's Scripturally Anchored** – not mystical guesswork.
2. **It's Prophetically Current** – briefings are updated monthly.

3. **It's Apostolically Legal** – decrees are courtroom-ready.
4. **It's Plug-and-Play** – just read, pray, and obey.

The Vault is not about drama. It's about dominion.

✳ Tactical Decree Sample

Declaration: Sudden Interference in Contracts

"In the Name of Jesus, I issue a cease-and-desist order in the Courts of Heaven against all interference from familiar spirits, human agents, and monitoring demons. I sever every tongue that speaks sabotage. I call for the Angel of Justice to silence the accuser and restore what was stolen. I loose the sevenfold return from the thief and declare new contracts are being dispatched now, in Jesus' name!"

🧬 Customize the Vault to Your Industry

We are developing Warfare Vaults for:

- **Real Estate and Development**
- **Coaching and Consulting**
- **Healthcare and Wellness**
- **Finance and Investments**

- **Media and Content Creation**
- **Ministry and Nonprofits**

Every sector has specific attacks — and God has specific solutions.

Final Word

The Warfare Vault™ exists so you don't have to guess how to fight.
You were never meant to react.
You were meant to **rule**.

Let this vault be your arsenal.
Let your prayers be **legal, targeted, and prophetic**.
And let your company walk in the victory that's already been won.

Chapter 13

Commanding the Morning™ — Daily Prophetic Declarations for Executives and Intercessors

"Have you commanded the morning since your days began, and caused the dawn to know its place?"
— *Job 38:12*

Every new day is a battlefield.

And the question Heaven asks is not:

- "Did you check your email?"
- "Did you close that deal?"
- "Did you get to the gym?"

The real question is:
Did you command the morning?

🔲 What It Means to Command the Morning

To command the morning is to:

- Legally establish your spiritual jurisdiction before the enemy does
- Preemptively strike against demonic cycles
- Set your business, city, and staff in divine alignment
- Activate angels, blessings, and prophetic assignments for the day
- Cancel the devil's scheduling of destruction

Most believers wake up **in reaction**.
But Kingdom leaders wake up **in rulership**.

✳️ The Divine Order of the Day

Each day begins in the spirit long before the sun rises.

The devil tries to schedule:

- Accidents
- Delays
- Strife in staff meetings
- Missed emails
- Financial sabotage
- Witchcraft appointments

But Jesus taught us to **pray first** — not after.

That's what **Commanding the Morning™** is:
A **prophetic protocol** that executes Heaven's agenda at the beginning of every day.

🔊 What's Inside the Commanding the Morning™ Package

Each declaration package includes:

- **Daily warfare decrees** (PDF + audio format)
- **Prophetic phrase of the day** (to meditate on and speak out)

- **Activation prayer** (legal language to enforce God's will)
- **Angel assignment statements** (to deploy assistance)
- **Optional communion instructions** (to sanctify the day in covenant)

These are short, potent, and mobile-ready — ideal for:

- Morning commutes
- Pre-staff meetings
- Executive prayer circles
- Early riser intercessors
- Prophetic teams covering cities

🗣️ Sample Morning Command Decree

Day 12: Financial Flow and Divine Strategy

"I command this morning to yield financial fruit assigned to me from Heaven. I declare every demonic plug is removed, and every divine channel is open. Angels of commerce and provision, I authorize your deployment. Contracts, clients, and divine surprises — come forth now. Every word curse over my business is revoked. I move in strategy, not stress. This day is governed by grace and breakthrough. In Jesus' name."

🔄 How to Build a Morning Command Routine

1. **Wake before sunrise if possible** — this is when spiritual climates are most moldable.
2. **Take communion** — sanctify your business and body under the blood of Jesus.
3. **Speak out loud** — declarations shift atmospheres.
4. **Visualize the outcomes** — faith sees.
5. **Send angels intentionally** — use Scripture-based assignment statements.
6. **Journal prophetic insight** — record instructions or visions.

🧱 Brick-by-Brick: Each Day Builds the Wall

Commanding the Morning isn't a one-time fix.
It's a **daily building process**.

Like Nehemiah's wall, each declaration:

- Fortifies a gap
- Seals a breach
- Strengthens your gates
- Prepares you for what's ahead

Whether you're a CEO, intercessor, or both — this daily rhythm is your foundation of victory.

🚀 The Results of Commanding the Morning

Those who apply this prophetic discipline often experience:

- Fewer missed opportunities
- Supernatural insight before big decisions
- Protection from misaligned partnerships
- Timely phone calls and divine appointments
- Renewed focus and decreased chaos
- Consistent spiritual momentum

Why? Because **Heaven's order** has been enforced before the world's chaos can take root.

Final Word

In the end, every leader either wakes up to command the day — or spends the day recovering from what wasn't commanded.

Let your company be covered.
Let your team be led by light.

Let your life be governed by the Spirit — **from dawn till dominion**.

You were born to **command the morning**.

Chapter 14

The Prophetic CEO™ Model — Leading with Revelation, Not Just Strategy

"Surely the Lord God does nothing unless He reveals His secret to His servants the prophets."
—*Amos 3:7*

In today's turbulent world, leadership requires more than experience.
More than metrics.
More than management.

It requires **prophetic insight** — the kind that sees through fog, discerns hidden risks, and builds what Heaven is backing.

That's where the **Prophetic CEO™** comes in.

💼 The Age of the Prophetic Executive

A Prophetic CEO is not just a business leader.

They are:

- A watchman over their team
- A spiritual gatekeeper for their region
- A carrier of Heaven's vision into Earth's structures
- A strategic advisor, guided by the Holy Spirit
- An economic reformer, divinely positioned in the marketplace

You don't have to be weird. You have to be **wired into Heaven**.

✿ Characteristics of a Prophetic CEO

1. **Discerns seasons and shifts**
   a. Knows when to expand, contract, pivot, or protect
   b. Reads divine timing, not just market timing
2. **Makes decisions with divine intel**
   a. Asks, "What is Heaven saying?" before signing a deal
3. **Leads from the secret place**
   a. Spends as much time in prayer as in boardrooms
4. **Hosts God's presence in the workplace**

      a. Doesn't compartmentalize spirituality and business

5. **Builds for generational impact, not just quarterly gain**

      a. Thinks in covenants, not just contracts

🧠 Prophetic > Predictive

Data is helpful. Forecasts are fine.

But what happens when:

- The data is wrong?
- The forecast collapses?
- A crisis comes without warning?

Only revelation can override deception.

That's why prophetic leaders can survive what others can't.
They build on **the Rock**, not market trends.

🔄 From CEO to CPO (Chief Prayer Officer)

Every Prophetic CEO must also be a **Chief Prayer Officer**:

- Hosting daily communion with the Lord
- Covering staff, buildings, and contracts in prayer
- Submitting legal cases to the Courts of Heaven
- Partnering with intercessors for clarity and protection
- Receiving blueprints in dreams and confirming them in the Word

This is how you turn your company into a **Goshen Zone.**

🧱 Building a Kingdom-Driven Company

A Prophetic CEO lays these foundations:

- **Altar of Prayer**: A spiritual portal for Heaven's counsel
- **Word-Based Culture**: Bible verses on the walls and in the workflow
- **Prophetic Team Meetings**: Time for discernment, not just data
- **Heaven's Strategy Sessions**: Fasting, worship, intercession before big launches
- **Marketplace Discipleship**: Helping team members grow in Christ

Your company is not just a business. It's a **prophetic embassy**.

👥 Prophetic CEO Doesn't Mean "Solo Prophet"

Every prophetic CEO needs:

- Wise counsel (Proverbs 11:14)
- Prophetic advisors (2 Chronicles 20:20)
- Intercessory backup (like Aaron and Hur for Moses)
- Legal covering in the Courts of Heaven
- Apostolic alignment for sending and authority

This is a **team assignment**, not a lone-ranger anointing.

💡 Prophetic CEO Activation

Start your day by praying:

"Jesus, I surrender this company to Your Kingship.
Make me a prophetic steward of Heaven's wisdom.
Let every strategy be Spirit-breathed.
Let my decisions reflect divine timing.
Let Goshen protection cover every employee and client.
I declare I am a builder of Heaven's economy on Earth."

🚀 Final Word

In this hour, God is raising up CEOs who don't just run companies.
They **prophesy destinies**.
They **disciple nations**.
They **command wealth for righteous purposes**.

You are not just a business leader.
You are a **watchman in a suit**, a **shepherd in the boardroom**, and a **prophet at the gate**.

Welcome to the **Prophetic CEO™ era**.

Chapter 15

Installing a Spiritual Security Officer™ — How to Cover Your Business 24/7

"I have set watchmen on your walls, O Jerusalem;
They shall never hold their peace day or night."
— *Isaiah 62:6*

Every smart business has cybersecurity.

Every major corporation has physical security.

But how many companies have **spiritual security**?

Introducing the Spiritual Security Officer™ (SSO) — a new prophetic position created for a time when the war is **unseen**, but the consequences are **visible.**

It's time to **spiritually retrofit** your organization.

◐ What Is a Spiritual Security Officer™?

An SSO is a Kingdom-trained individual assigned to:

- Watch, pray, and war over the business environment
- Intercede for leadership decisions, contracts, and timelines
- Discern and confront spiritual attacks before they manifest
- Cover teams, meetings, and clients with strategic decrees
- Apply Courts of Heaven protocols for disputes and injustices
- Work in sync with the executive team — like a spiritual COO

This isn't superstition. It's **proactive Kingdom governance.**

🧠 Why You Need an SSO Now

We are in a marketplace war zone:

- New Age witchcraft is embedded in HR trainings
- Demonic networks release hexes over entrepreneurs
- Freemasonry and occult roots defile land, cities, and buildings
- Surveillance culture opens doors for digital oppression
- Sorcery disguised as "mindfulness" is pushed on your staff

If you're not guarding your gates, **the enemy already is**.

🔐 What an SSO Actually Does

Daily:

- Opens and closes the business in prayer
- Speaks daily decrees (Commanding the Morning™ style)
- Walks the premises physically or in the spirit
- Guards entry points (physical, spiritual, relational)

Weekly:

- Audits the environment for demonic cycles or emotional disruptions
- Reviews prayer requests from staff or leadership
- Seeks Heaven's strategy for upcoming projects

Monthly:

- Files Courts of Heaven petitions for key legal matters
- Discerns atmosphere shifts in the region
- Deploys angels via prophetic acts and Scripture

📋 What to Look for in an SSO Candidate

Not everyone who prays qualifies.

Look for someone who is:

- Spiritually mature and rooted in Scripture
- Prophetically sensitive but not emotionally unstable
- Teachable, trustworthy, and understands confidentiality
- Bold in intercession and legal prayer
- Comfortable interacting with executives and cleaning the air spiritually

This is **not a pulpit role** — it's a **hidden frontlines assignment**.

🏷 The Certification Track

Our **SSO Certification Program** includes:

- 4-Week Online Training (Video + PDF Workbook)
- Real-Life Case Studies: "When Witchcraft Infiltrated a Boardroom"
- Altar-Building Templates for Businesses
- Sample Legal Petitions for Common Attacks
- LinkedIn Badge + Printable Certificate for Display

Certified SSOs are marked as **Watchmen of the Marketplace**.

🔁 How to Integrate an SSO Into Your Business

1. **Appoint with clarity** — give them recognized authority in the spirit.
2. **Schedule regular check-ins** — spiritual intelligence belongs at the strategy table.
3. **Invite them to pray before major decisions or launches.**
4. **Cover the SSO in prayer and compensation.**

5. **Treat them as part of your prophetic ecosystem — not an afterthought.**

💼 Case Study Snapshot

Company: Faith-Focused Design Firm
Problem: Missed deals, team conflict, strange delays
SSO Hired: Prayed, discerned occult presence tied to previous tenant
Action: Cleansed space, broke land covenants, filed Courts of Heaven case
Result: Peace returned, deals closed, unity restored

Spiritual interference was **invisible until confronted —** and the SSO made the difference.

Commissioning Prayer for SSOs

"Father, I anoint this servant to stand watch over this company.
May they see what You see, hear what You whisper, and say what You command.
May no unclean spirit pass their post, and no strategy of hell go undetected.
Let Heaven's counsel, protection, and verdicts flow through their watch.

In Jesus' name, this SSO is commissioned — for Your glory and the safety of this business."

Final Word

We don't just need managers.
We need **gatekeepers**.
We don't just need executives.
We need **intercessors in armor**.

Every righteous company must have someone who says:

"Not on my watch."

Chapter 16

From Babylon to Goshen — Breaking Free from the Cursed Economy

"Come out of her, My people, so that you will not share in her sins or receive any of her plagues."
— *Revelation 18:4*

Babylon is not just a place.
It's a system — an invisible economy designed to enslave.

It rewards compromise.
It disguises corruption as success.
It exalts greed and calls it growth.
It props up the wicked and mocks the righteous.

And it's the dominant operating system of most businesses today.

But God is calling His people — and their companies — **out of Babylon and into Goshen**.

💣 Babylon's Economic Traps

1. **Debt Dependence** – Where bondage is marketed as opportunity
2. **Predatory Partnerships** – Where alliances serve darkness for short-term gain
3. **Greed-Driven Metrics** – Where success is measured by size, not spirit
4. **Occult Gatekeepers** – Where advancement requires bowing to hidden thrones
5. **Sorcery Over Strategy** – Where manifestation, energy, and false light replace prayer and prophecy

Babylon always comes with a cost: **your soul, your voice, your legacy**.

🔥 The Cursed Currency

The money of Babylon is spiritually defiled.

- It's backed by **bloodshed, theft**, and **global manipulation**
- It's used to **fund injustice** and **finance idolatry**
- It carries **judgments** unless it's **cleansed by covenant**

This is why many Christians have money... but no rest.
Success... but no legacy.
Revenue... but no revelation.

You can't partner with Babylon and expect Goshen's covering.

🛑 Babylon in the Boardroom

When companies unknowingly align with Babylon, they experience:

- Repeated cycles of **loss** and **invisible resistance**

- Sudden **employee sabotage** or **infighting**
- Contracts that **collapse at the last minute**
- **Clients or investors** with hidden demonic ties
- An atmosphere of **chaos, confusion, and compromise**

These are not "market forces."
They are **spiritual indicators** of a compromised economy.

✦ Goshen's Economy: Kingdom Principles in Action

In contrast, Goshen companies walk in:

1. **Covenant Wealth** – Money that obeys Kingdom laws
2. **Justice-Based Revenue** – Profit without compromise
3. **Prophetic Partnership** – Relationships aligned with God's vision
4. **Righteous Inheritance** – Growth rooted in legacy, not lust
5. **Spiritual Firewalls** – Protection against backlash, collapse, or demonic cycles

Goshen isn't just safety — it's **strategy and sovereignty**.

🔓 Breaking Free from Babylon

To come out of Babylon, you must:

- **Repent** for all partnerships, practices, and profits built on compromise
- **Renounce** covenants with Mammon, Freemasonry, or occult frameworks
- **Realign** your company with Kingdom values: justice, holiness, integrity
- **Reform** your systems: hiring, marketing, investing, and management
- **Reestablish** your financial gates through altars of righteousness

This is deliverance at the corporate level.

🧱 Building a Goshen Company

It's not enough to reject Babylon — you must **build Goshen**:

- Install prayer covering (SSO model)
- Engage Courts of Heaven monthly
- Tithe righteously — not just personally, but corporately

- Fund justice, deliverance, and Kingdom advancement
- Submit major decisions to prophetic counsel
- Host the Holy Spirit in your office and boardroom

Goshen businesses don't just **survive shaking** — they **shine in it.**

👀 Heaven Is Watching

Every CEO, founder, and investor must answer this:

Will your company bow to Babylon's system... or build Goshen's standard?

Because judgment is already falling on unjust wealth. And the Lord is looking for **trustworthy stewards** to transfer Kingdom resources to.

The choice isn't just moral — it's **survival.**
And Goshen isn't just safe — it's **set apart to rule.**

Chapter 17

Kingdom Wealth and the End-Time Transfer

"The wealth of the wicked is stored up for the righteous."
— *Proverbs 13:22*

💰 The Wealth Shift Has Already Begun

We are not waiting for a wealth transfer.
It's already in motion.

God is rerouting resources.
He is bankrupting Babylon.
He is shaking corrupted systems so that only Kingdom structures remain standing.

The end-time wealth transfer is **not about luxury** — it's about **assignment**.

🔍 Why the Transfer Must Happen

1. **To fund the Gospel to the ends of the earth**
2. **To rebuild Kingdom infrastructure in every mountain of culture**
3. **To expose and dismantle the systems of Mammon and injustice**
4. **To restore what was stolen through slavery, colonization, corruption, and sorcery**
5. **To glorify Jesus, not celebrities or billionaires**

God is not looking for hoarders.
He's looking for **Holy Ghost financiers**.

🏠 What Wealth Really Is

Wealth is not just money.

In the Kingdom, **wealth includes**:

- Revelation
- Relationships
- Real estate
- Resources

- Righteous strategies
- Reach (influence and distribution)

A righteous remnant is being trained now to steward **multi-dimensional wealth** — not just make money, but multiply impact under Heaven's direction.

🔐 Who Qualifies for the Transfer?

Those who:

- Walk in **integrity** before God
- Are **delivered** from greed, pride, and self-glory
- **Tithe** and give sacrificially in faith
- Build **altars of obedience**, not platforms of ego
- Understand the **spiritual war over economics**
- Are aligned with **apostolic and prophetic oversight**

The Lord will not entrust His treasuries to those still flirting with Babylon.

💣 The Battle Over Money Is Spiritual

Satan is fighting the wealth transfer because:

- He uses money to enslave, distract, and corrupt

- He funds witchcraft, abortion, trafficking, and false religion
- He fears what will happen if the righteous are resourced
- He knows money moves governments, media, and policy

That's why **business intercession** is non-negotiable.

Without prayer and prophetic insight, your finances remain vulnerable to manipulation.

📊 Signs of a Coming Transfer

Watch for:

- Sudden collapses of corrupt financial empires
- Strange exposure of hidden elite wealth
- Revival hubs attracting investment without asking
- Goshen businesses thriving while Babylon burns
- Whistleblowers revealing the truth about currency, gold, crypto, and global manipulation
- Transfer of intellectual property, land, tech, and platforms to Kingdom hands

It's not just cash. It's **control of the gates**.

🔧 How to Prepare Your Business

1. **Clean your house**: remove any compromised partnerships, unjust systems, or agreements with darkness
2. **Consecrate your finances**: tithe, give firstfruits, sow prophetically
3. **Align your mission**: make sure your company is building Heaven's priorities, not just chasing trends
4. **Install covering**: build a prayer altar, assign intercessors, engage Courts of Heaven
5. **Stay ready**: when the shaking begins, be positioned to receive the spoils (like Israel at the Red Sea)

This is **Goshen economy in action.**

📢 Prophetic Decree

"I declare I am a trusted steward of Kingdom wealth.
The gates of Babylon are falling.
The vaults of injustice are opening.
And the transfer is coming to those aligned with the Lamb.
My company will be a distribution center of righteousness.
My heart is clean.

My hands are ready.
My purpose is prophetic.
In Jesus' name, I receive the assignment of Kingdom wealth."

Appendices

Appendix A: Court of Heaven Petitions for Business Warfare

These are pre-written legal petitions designed for use in the Courts of Heaven, addressing:

- Financial loss and theft
- Wrongful staffing decisions
- Contractual betrayal
- Occult interference and curses
- Regional demonic agreements

Each petition is rooted in Scripture, formatted with legal language, and includes:

- A plea for the blood of Jesus
- Renunciations of agreement with darkness
- Requests for angelic enforcement and restitution

- Decrees for overturning demonic verdicts
- Closing judgments with thanksgiving and praise

Appendix B: Daily Declarations for Business Leaders and Intercessors

This appendix provides a full month (30 days) of strategic, Scripture-based declarations:

- Identity and authority in Christ for the marketplace
- Clarity, wisdom, and discernment
- Open doors and divine appointments
- Protection from witchcraft, sabotage, and demonic cycles
- Acceleration in assignments and fulfillment of destiny

Formatted for easy reading aloud, daily or as part of a group, these declarations help enforce Kingdom rule in any business environment.

Appendix C: Goshen Region Mapping Template

This visual and strategic tool helps intercessors and CEOs:

- Map their city or region for spiritual strongholds
- Identify known or suspected demonic gates (e.g., altars, Masonic lodges, high places)
- Track prophetic dreams and insights
- Mark known covenant-breaking locations (e.g., abortion clinics, witchcraft centers)
- Design prayer walks, angelic dispatches, and prophetic acts

The template is printable and editable, designed for repeated monthly use.

Appendix D: Prophetic Risk Audit Workbook

A spiritual forensic workbook designed to uncover:

- Legal rights demons may have to operate in your business
- Generational curses attached to leadership or location
- Employee open doors (occult practices, sin, rebellion)
- Repeating negative patterns and cycles
- Missed assignments or neglected prayer coverage

Each audit includes:

- Discernment questions
- Scriptural reference points
- Repentance protocols
- Closing declarations and prayer directives

Appendix E: Certification Model for SSO (Spiritual Security Officer)

A turnkey model to train, commission, and deploy certified **Spiritual Security Officers™** in the workplace, including:

- A 4-week course curriculum
- Case studies and real-world testimonies
- Templates for prayer altars, watchman rotations, and employee protection plans
- LinkedIn badge, printable certificate, and digital credential
- Guidelines for CEOs to recognize, empower, and activate SSOs in their organization

This appendix includes onboarding, sample modules, and ongoing growth strategies.

Made in the USA
Columbia, SC
29 June 2025

60016752R20063